Stewardship of God's Grace

The true Gospel of God entrusted to you!

Rudi Louw

Copyright © 2014 by Rudi Louw Publishing

All rights reserved solely by the author. No part of this book may be reproduced in any form *without the permission of the author.*

Most Scripture quotations are taken from the *Revised Standard Version*, Holy Bible, Thomas Nelson Publishers. Copyright © 1983 by Thomas Nelson, Inc.

Some Scripture quotations were taken from the *New King James Version*, Holy Bible, Thomas Nelson Publishers. Copyright © 1983 by Thomas Nelson, Inc.

All Scripture quotations not taken from the RSV, NKJV or Mirror Bible are a literal translation of the Scriptures.

The Holy Scriptures are just that, HOLY.

Statements enclosed in brackets were inserted into Scripture quotations to add emphasis or clarify the meaning of what is being said in those scriptures. The integrity of God's Word to man was not compromised in any way. Due care and diligence was cautiously exercised to keep the Word of Truth intact.

For example: The apostle Paul said in his second letter to Timothy in chapter three verse sixteen that: *"All Scripture is given by inspiration of God* (literally God breathed), *and is profitable for doctrine, for reproof, for correction, for instruction **in righteousness**,"* NKJV

Content

The marvel of the Holy Bible ………..5

Acknowledgement ………………13

Foreword ……………………..15

Prayer ……………………...25

1. *God trusts us to be faith-full!* ……...29
2. *I Judge no one!* ………………35
3. *God concluded His Judgment of us in the Death of Christ!* ……………....53
4. *Much is given!* …………………61
5. *Sing O Barren One!* ……………73
6. *God's image and inscription* ………78
7. *Be a good steward!* ……………...81
8. *Necessity is laid upon us!* …………91
9. *Boldness & Confidence!* …………101
10. *Take your place!* ………………109
11. *The content of our message!* …..121

12. *Fully embrace God's Word in your heart!* 127

13. *Abide in Him so you can bear much fruit!* 133

About the author 147

The marvel of the Holy Bible

1. The *theme* and *inspired thought* of Scripture continues *uninterrupted*.

It took *1,500 years* to compile the Holy Bible, involving *more than 40 different authors*, yet the theme and inspired thought of Scripture continues *uninterrupted*, from author to author, from beginning till end.

2. Absence *of mythical stories:*

Compare philosophies and theories about creation in the Middle East, Europe, Asia, Africa and Latin America, and you'll find mythical scenarios, gods feuding and cutting up other gods to form the heavens and the earth. In ancient Greek mythology, the Greeks see Atlas carrying the earth on his shoulders. In India, Hindus believe 8 elephants carry the earth on their backs.

But in contrast, Job, the oldest book in the Holy Bible, declares that *God suspends the earth 'on nothing.' (Job 26:7)*

This was said millennia before Isaac Newton discovered the invisible laws of gravity that delicately balance every planet and sun in its individual circuit.

In contrast to every other ancient attempt to give a creation account, *the Holy Bible pictures the creation of the earth in a very scientific manner.*

In Gen 1 for instance, the continents are lifted from the seas, then vegetation is formed and later, animal life, all reproducing *'according to its own kind,'* **thus recognising the fixed genetic laws.**

Finally we have the bringing forth of man and woman, *all done by God in a dignified and proper manner, without mythological adornments.*

The rest of the Holy Bible follows suit.

The narratives are **true historical documents**, *faithfully reflecting society and culture,* **as history and archaeology would discover them thousands of years later. Not only is the Holy Bible historically accurate, it is also reliable when it deals with scientific subjects.**

It was not written as a textbook on history, science, mathematics or medicine, *yet, when its writers touch on these subjects,* **they often state facts that scientific advancement would not reveal or even consider until thousands of years later.**

While many have doubted the accuracy of the Holy Bible, time and continued research have consistently demonstrated that the Word of God is better informed than its critics.

3. The Holy Bible is *intact*.

Of all the ancient works of substantial size, *the Holy Bible against all odds and expectations survives intact.*

Compared with other ancient writings, the Holy Bible has more manuscripts as evidence to support it than any ten pieces of classical literature combined!

The plays of William Shakespeare, for instance, were written about four hundred years ago, and written after the invention of the printing press. Many of his original words have been lost in numerous sections, *yet the Holy Bible's uncanny preservation has weathered thousands of years of wars, contradictions, persecutions, fires and invasions.*

Jewish scribes, **like no other manuscript has ever been preserved**, *preserved the Holy Bible's Old Covenant text through centuries.* **They kept tabs on every letter, syllable, word and paragraph**.

They continued from generation to generation to appoint and train special classes of men within their culture **whose sole duty it was to preserve and transmit these documents <u>with perfect accuracy and fidelity</u>**.

Who ever bothered to count the letters, syllables, or words of Plato, Aristotle or Seneca for that matter?

When it comes to the New Testament, the actual number of preserved manuscripts is so great that it becomes overwhelming.

There are more than 5,680 Greek manuscripts, more than 10,000 Latin Vulgate manuscripts and at least 9,300 other versions; there exist a further 25,000 manuscript copies of portions of the New Testament.

No other document of antiquity even begins to approach such numbers.

The closest in comparison is Homer's <u>Iliad</u> with only 643 manuscripts. The first complete work of Homer only dates back to the 13th century.

4. In dealing with time, the Holy Bible *accurately foretells what will happen ahead of time, with unmatched results*.

No other ancient work even begins to attempt this.

Other books claim divine inspiration, such as the Koran, the Book of Mormon, and parts of the Veda.

But none of these books contains predictive foretelling.

This one fact we know for certain, and it is undeniable: *While microscopic scrutiny would show up the imperfections, blemishes and defects of any work of man, <u>it magnifies the beauties and perfection of God</u>, just as every flower displays in accurate detail, the reflection and perfection of beauty, <u>so does the Word of Truth when it is scrutinized</u>.*

Historian, Philip Schaff wrote:

'...Without money and weapons, Jesus the Christ conquered more millions, than Alexander, Caesar, Mohammed and Napoleon.

Without science and learning, He (Jesus the Christ) shed more light on things human and divine than all philosophers and scholars combined.

Without the eloquence of schools, He (Jesus the Christ) spoke such words of life as was never spoken before or since and produced effects, which lie beyond the reach of orator or poet.

Without writing a single line, He (Jesus the Christ) set more pens in motion, and furnished themes for more sermons, orations, discussions, learned volumes, works of art, and songs of praise, **than the whole army of great men of ancient and modern times combined**.*'* (The person of Christ, p33. 1913)

Today, there are literally billions of Bibles in more than 2,000 languages,

…isn't it about time you find out what it really has to say?

Hey listen, the Holy Bible is all about Jesus, the Messiah, the Christ,

…and everything about Jesus Christ is really about YOU!!

Study Tips:

Read 2 Corinthians 5:14, 16, 18, 19, and 21.

In the light of these Scriptures it should be obvious that if you want to study the Holy Bible,

...you should study it in the light of mankind's Redemption!

Daily feed on Redemption Realities found in the book of Acts, Romans 1 through 8, Ephesians, Colossians, Galatians, 1Peter 1, 2Peter 1, James 1, 1 and 2Corinthians.

Acknowledgement

I want to acknowledge and thank one of my mentors in the faith, Francois du Toit, for blessing and impacting my life with revelation knowledge.

The portion on *"The marvel of the Holy Bible"* was borrowed from his website: http://www.mirrorword.net/ as students so often feel they have a right to do with things that come from teachers they respect. Just as Galatians 6:6 says: *"Let him who is taught the Word **share in all good things** with him who teaches."*

To all our dear friends and family, and to all those who helped me with this project,

…but especially to my wife Carmen,

…for all the love and support, and for being my partner in this adventurous life,

THANK YOU!

Foreword

Thank you for taking the time to read this book.

Let me start off by saying that *I am totally addicted to my Daddy's love for me;*

…I am in love with Jesus Christ, *and that is enough for me!*

The love of God is so much more than a doctrine, a philosophy, or a theory; it is so much more and goes so much deeper than knowledge; *it way surpasses knowledge,*

…we are talking heart language here,

…therefore this book was not written to impress intellectuals with knowledge and philosophy, theologians with theories and doctrine, nor English majors with grammar and spelling for that matter,

…so if you come up with any other definitions or find any language inaccuracies please don't use it to disqualify Love's own message I bring to you in this book.

I write *to impact people's hearts;*

...to make them see the mysteries that has been hidden in Father God's heart, concerning Christ Jesus, and really *concerning THEM,* so as to arrest their conscience with it, *that I may introduce them to their original design, and to their true selves;* **and present them to themselves perfect in Christ Jesus,**

*...and set them apart unto Him **in love**,* as a chaste virgin,

We are involved with the biggest romance of the ages;

...therefore this book cannot be read as you would a novel; *casually.* It is not a cleverly devised little myth or fable.

It contains revelation and *truth* into some things you may or may not have considered before. It is not blasphemy or error though.

It is the TRUTH of God, ultimate TRUTH, and therefore has direct bearing upon YOUR life, **the Word and the Spirit is my witness** *to the reality of these things!*

Be like the people of Berea the apostle Paul ministered to in Acts 17:11. Open yourself up to study the revelation contained in this book, *to see if these things are **true and real**.*

...but be forewarned, do not become guilty of the sins of the Pharisees, ***or you too will miss***

out on the depth of fulfillment God Himself, who is LOVE, wants to give you.

(Jesus said of the Pharisees and Sadducees that they strain out every little gnat BUT swallow whole camels. What He meant by that is that *some people seem to have it all together when it comes to doctrine and they love to argue.*

It makes them feel important, but it is nothing other than EMPTY religious and intellectual pride.

They know the Scriptures in and out, and YET they are still so IGNORANT about **REAL TRUTH that is only found in LOVE;**

...they are still so ignorant and indifferent **towards the things that REALLY MATTERS.**

They are always arguing over the use of *every little jot and tittle* and over the meaning and interpretation of *every word of Scripture.*

The exact thing they accuse everyone else of doing though; the precise thing they judge everyone else for, *they are actually doing themselves,* that is: **they often completely misinterpret and twist what is being said, *making a big deal of insignificant things,***

...while obscuring or weakening God's real truth; the truth of His LOVE

*They are always majoring on minors, **because they do not understand the heart of God***

***…and therefore they constantly miss the whole point of the message**.)*

Paul himself said it so beautifully:

*"…the letter kills but **the Spirit BRINGS LIFE**;"*

*"…<u>knowledge puffs up</u>, but **LOVE EDIFIES**."*

I say again:

Allow yourself to get caught up in the revelation I am about to share.

Open yourself up to study the insight contained in this book *not only with a desire to gain knowledge, but also with anticipation **to hear from Father God yourself**;*

…to encounter Him through His Word;

…and to embrace truth, in order to know and believe the LOVE God has for <u>you</u>,

*…so that you may get so caught up in it, **that you too may receive from Him; LOVES' impartation of LIFE***

*If you take heed to these things, and yield yourself fully to it, **it is custom designed and guaranteed to forever alter and enrich your life!***

"We make it our aim
to be well pleasing to Him,"

"We are totally engaged
in the loveliness
of that which is
of exceedingly great value;"

"Whether we are in
a physical union with our
bodies or a spiritual union
with our source;
it makes no difference
to God's esteem of us!"

" We already have His favor!"

"...for we already stand
face to face
with God's judgment of us
in Christ,

as if we are looking at a
snapshot of what happened
and of what was revealed there,

...so that each one of us
may receive
the things in Him we deserve

based on what has been
manifested
and openly declared
concerning us
in Christ's seat of authority!

...and based on our embrace
of that truth!"

"This has nothing to do
with what we've experienced
in our individual lives,
...whether we've encountered
amazingly good things,

*...or partaken of
meaningless bad things."*

*"We now persuade people
concerning the radiance
of the Lord,*

*...of His truth
and of His love
and of His person,*

*and of your own person
revealed there in Him!"*

"We are well acquainted with His visible glory,

...and it is therefore now also mirrored in us!"

"We are well known to God,

...our lives are transparent before Him,"

"...and we anticipate the echo of truth in you as you witness our lives

and as we relate to you
the good news!"

"We are confident that
that transparency of innocence
will rub off on your conscience
and be imparted to you as
well!"

- 2Corinthians 5:9 to 11

Prayer

Father thank you that *You have an eternal purpose* **for every one of us.**

Father we see this time *of our connecting with Your thoughts* here in this book, not as an insignificant time.

Father we refuse to handle *the sacred intimate deep things of God revealed to us in Christ Jesus*

…as just mere information or just more sentimental religious nonsense,

…or cleverly devised myths and fables by which to have our ears tickled and to be entertained,

…and to afterwards **still refuse to appropriate it,**

…and yet feel blessed to have read about it in this book!

Father, we mean business with You, o God; **We mean business with Your Word, Father.**

We bow down before You *right now in our hearts,*

...before Your love,

...and before the lordship of Your truth.

God we ask that You would **so work in our hearts through your Word;**

...through Your revelation of redemption revealed in Your Scriptures and therefore in this book,

Father we ask that You would so work in our hearts *through that revelation*

...that You would **release us in our inner-man,**

...that we will find ourselves even in these next few days and in this coming week *living in a new dimension,*

*...living **in Your energy** to a greater degree,*

...so that we can with a new freedom and boldness testify to the world around us *of the truth of your Word;*

...of the integrity of your love and of the integrity of Your promises.

Father thank you, that in dealing with Your Word of truth,

...in dealing with Jesus Christ,

...in dealing with the work of redemption,

...we are no longer dealing with mere post-dated promises!

But Father we are dealing *with reality!*

We are dealing, not with promises for the future, *or with maybes!*

We are dealing with what You have decreed concerning us, *and then accomplished in Christ Jesus,*

...*in that marvelous, successful work of redemption!*

Thank you Father for the total restoration of man, in Christ Jesus!

*...and that **we have been entrusted with the truth of this gospel!***

*...**with good news Father!***

Lord I thank you that *You came to set us free*

*...**so we can be truly free!***

Lord set us free by Your truth *as we engage You; as we read Your revelation!*

Thank you for setting us free **from everything that binds us up and holds us back, *or restricts us from that freedom!***

...from living that abundant life Jesus talked about;

...being strong Christians,

...strong witnesses for You!

Thank you Father for every person You drew to read this book by Your Spirit!

Thank you that You drew them **so that You can draw them into seeing and believing the truth of Your Gospel**,

...and so that You can draw them unto You,

...into sweet friendship and fellowship,

...and into strong agreement with You Father!

And we pray that the **anointing of the Holy Spirit** *will break through into every person's heart*

...and liberate us even more with Your truth and with Your power!

...Father, even people that have been living in deep darkness, people that have been living in all kinds of bondage!

Liberate in this book *and through Your* **revelation Lord.**

In Jesus mighty name! Amen!

Chapter 1

God trusts us to be faith-full!

I want to share with you on the subject of: *THE STEWARDSHIP OF GOD'S GRACE.*

I believe it will prove to be a tremendous challenge to you *as you realize that God entrusts us <u>with His Word</u>,*

...yes you included!

Isn't it nice when someone trusts you?

Ha... ha... ha...

Listen, suspicion comes from the enemy!

Trust and faith comes from God.

God does not encourage suspicion!

God encourages trust and faith!

There is no suspicion *within the fellowship* of the Godhead; *within the fellowship of the Trinity!*

Neither is there suspicion from out of the Godhead; from out of God's triune being *towards us!*

Hallelujah!

God doesn't accommodate any suspicion in His own heart!

Suspicion isn't tolerated in Heaven!

God does not encourage suspicion!

God encourages trust and faith!

That is exactly why God designed a new covenant that legally destroys any reference to our past.

God does not keep an account of your past!

...because it would only feed suspicion!

He says,

"I will no longer be mindful of your transgressions ...because of the blood of My Son Jesus Christ."

God wants our relationship with Him to be a relationship *of mutual trust ...where we trust Him,* **and wherein He can trust us,**

...and entrust us with His grace!

God is looking for **faith-full** people *that He can trust!*

…not faith-empty people! Amen!

Ha… ha… ha…

Are you a faithful person?

Are you standing steadfast in *the* faith?

Are you totally persuaded in *the faith of God that has once and for all been revealed and delivered to us in Christ Jesus?*

Because strong faith *can only come through revelation into these things, amen!*

Are you holding on to that revelation from God, **of Himself and of us, which He Himself has given us in Christ Jesus?**

*…and allowing it to be **your total focus?***

Your total focus is the only way for that revelation *to sustain you in these things,*

*…**and to keep you steadfast in the faith,***

*…**to sustain that faith,***

*…**and that strength within you!***

Can God trust you?

Can He entrust you with something *and know that you will be faithful with it?*

Are you trust-worthy?

Because you see, **maintaining your focus in God's revelation of Himself and of you in Christ Jesus is of the utmost importance!**

It has everything to do with your trust-worthiness!

...in relationship with Him,

...and in ministering to others!

God wants to speak that Word into us *that will sustain us in these things,*

...that Word of revelation that will become **a treasure** to us *that we hold on to and refuse to let go of,*

...that precious Word *straight from His heart,*

...*that will cause us to fall in love with Him and become addicted to His love and His truth!*

...so that our trust-worthiness *will no longer be dependent on ourselves,*

...on our own efforts and works,

*…but it will be **the fruit** of His revelation,*

*…**imparted** to our understanding and to our spirit!*

God wants to be *the One, who strengthens us with might in our inner-man,*

…and sustains us in that trust-worthiness,

*…as the Word of Christ gains entrance into our hearts **and begins to dwell in us richly!***

Hey, that is wisdom that is from above!

God wants His Word and His revelation of Himself and of us in Christ Jesus *to be received,*

…so that it might find root in our lives and produce a harvest according to His purpose!

That is our stewardship!

Let's begin by reading together from Luke chapter twelve.

Chapter 2

I judge no one!

Luke 12:47

*"And **that servant who knew his Master's will**"*

...*not the one walking ignorantly, but the one **who knows his Master's will!***

And we know our Master's will, how?

Through His Word!

Through that revelation of Himself and of us in Christ Jesus!

...***through redemption truth!***

...***because His Word,*** (Christ Jesus, the eternal Word; the eternal thoughts of God concerning Himself and concerning us, made flesh) ***is the expression of His will!***

...***and that will is being testified to in the Scriptures!***

So it says,

*"...that servant who knew his Master's will, but did not make ready or act according to His will **shall receive a severe beating**."*

Now I know that it's not pleasant to read or talk about judgment of any kind;

...about the inevitable consequences to disobedience;

...about the inevitable consequence to the violation of truth,

...but there is a very real judgment in these things according to the Word of God

...and according to the promise of God!

I know God judged His Son over 2014 years ago now, with our transgressions and our iniquities,

...and for us who embrace redemption realities, we have passed from judgment to justification, from death to life,

...but listen carefully now, Jesus could not possibly bear your deliberate ignoring of redemption realities; your deliberate violation of truth;

...your deliberate disobedience to the will of God; to the New Covenant!

Matthew 7:21-23 confirms this.

Verse 23 makes it clear that He will say,

"...**depart from Me. I never knew you!**"

...and He is referring to those,

"...*who deliberately practice lawlessness!*"

The only sin today that man will ever stand guilty for *and that will carry its own inevitable Judgment;*

...its own inevitable consequence,

...is the sin of not accepting; the sin of rejecting the lordship of Jesus Christ;

...the supreme eminence of the One who is Truth Personified;

...the absolute clarity and fullness and supremacy of that eternal truth; that ultimate truth, revealed in Him, concerning us,

...concerning our original design and our true identity revealed and redeemed and fully restored to us in Him!

...and **"if we know His will and do not act according to His will,"**

Jesus Himself says here in Luke that,

"...**we will receive a severe beating**."

He goes on to say that,

"...he who did not know, but did what deserves a beating shall receive a light beating."

So obviously there are different degrees of judgment; **different degrees of consequences,** not from Jesus himself, not from God our Father, but from other spiritual forces, according to this Scripture

You should read what Jesus had to say there in that whole passage of Luke 12:35-48 for yourself.

It is a very sobering thing to realize that *we are all; every believer is considered His ministers,*

...and that when the truth comes to us, *something is required of us,*

...and that we *cannot afford* to be casual about it,

...or else we too will not escape the consequences of disobedience; the consequences of violating our conscience!

No one can live in violation of truth and get away with it!

The actual practical consequences are severe and inevitable!

Obviously Jesus is using a figure of speech here *and doesn't refer to Him or the Father beating up on anyone, and giving some people a severe beating, nor do they plan on literally cutting anyone in two!*

Ha…. Ha… ha… thank you Jesus!

Romans 8:1 says,

"There is now no condemnation (From Jesus or the Father,) *for those who are in Christ Jesus!"*

…and verse 31 says that,

"…If God is for us, who can be against us!"

*…**and He is for us** amen!*

Verse 33 says,

"Who then shall bring a charge (before God) *against God's elect? **It is God who justifies!***

Verse 34 says,

"Who is he who condemns? (Is it the Father? NO! He already dealt with that question in verse 33. Is it Christ then? NO!) *…It is Christ who died, and furthermore is also raised, who is even at the right hand of God* (united; together with the Father), *making intersession* (or intervention) *for us!"*

Verse 35,

"Who then shall separate us from the love of Christ?" (NO ONE!)

So, obviously Jesus is not referring to any kind of beating coming from Himself, nor His Father, when he talks about *those who do what deserves a beating.*

He also talks about consequences so severe that He refers to them *being cut asunder, or cut in two and their portion ripped away from them and them finding themselves in a place where they have everything in common with the unbelievers; they find themselves among the unbelievers,*

...reaping from the flesh corruption, not from God!

He is using a parable *to try and communicate to His disciples* **the inevitable ongoing consequences of violating your own heart in disobedience to truth.**

He is trying to relate to them that these consequences is just as severe as if you were to violate the law of gravity and jump off of a roof!

He is expressing to them *His total displeasure with the practice of* **ignoring the truth** *...and His disappointment and frustration and anguish over* **the deliberate violation of truth,**

...because of His great love for people, and wanting to spare them the negative consequences that is produces in the life of the individual and in this world because of these things,

...because of either ignoring God's truth or deliberately violating the truth of God we already know!!

We might as well face it; *He cannot be pleased with these things!*

That's why He is expressing such strong emotions as displeasure and severe disappointment, and utter frustration, and total anguish of heart!

...because what humanity still do not understand is that many of these consequences of disobedience **will carry through into the future,**

...even having its affects upon them past this life!

But I don't want you to understand me wrong right now.

I have already made it clear that neither God the Father not Jesus has any judgment in their heart towards you! *Jesus is not waiting for you with a whip up in Heaven!*

Ha… ha… ha…

The Father is not up there ready to Judge you and beat you with many stripes *or with even just a few!*

So relax, Max... ha... ha... ha...!

I can see I'm going to have to clarify myself some more, so turn with me in your Bible to John chapter five.

In John 5:22 & 23 Jesus makes it clear,

"For the Father Himself <u>judges no one</u>, but has committed all judgment to the Son."

"...that all should honor the Son, just as they honor the Father."

"He who does not honor the Son, does not honor the Father who sent Him"

John 3:17-19 say,

*"For God **did not send His Son into the world <u>to condemn the world</u>,** but that the world through Him might be saved"*

*"He who believes in Him is not condemned; but he who does not believe **is condemned already**..."*

John does not say that that person is now condemned by the Father *or by Jesus* for that matter!

No!

He goes on to say that that person *is condemned by his own unbelief and violation of truth!*

*"...**because he has not believed**..."*

That person remains trapped in darkness and bound by the law of sin and death *and all its inevitable consequences in the now and in the future!*

...because he or she refuses to believe and therefore chooses sin!

That very choice is sin, *it missis the mark*, and it inevitably leads to sin!

Verse 19 says,

"This is the condemnation;

...the light has come into the world,

...and yet some loved darkness rather than light, because their deeds were evil!"

Another translation says,

...and yet some loved darkness rather than light,

...and* (therefore) *their deeds were evil!"

In John 5:30 Jesus said,

"As I hear I judge; and my judgment is righteous, *because I do not seek My own will but the will of the Father who sent Me."*

What He meant was:

"You can't hide anything from Me! As I hear, I discern, and my discernment is accurate, because I know the truth revealed by the Father; I know the will of the Father"

Still, He makes it clear in John 8 and John 12 that **He refuses to be our judge.**

The father is not judging anyone, *and neither is Jesus!*

He said to the Pharisees,

John 8:15

*"**You judge** according to the flesh;"*

"I judge no one!"

In John 12 He makes it clear to them,

John 12:44-48

"Then Jesus cried out and said, 'He who believes in Me, believes not in Me but in Him who sent Me.'

*"...and **he who sees Me sees Him who sent Me**."*

*"I have come as a light into the world, **that whoever believes in Me should not abide in darkness**."*

*"...and if anyone hears My words and does not believe, **I do not judge him**:"*

*"...for **I did not come to judge the world**, but to save the world."*

*"He who rejects Me, and does not receive My words, **has that which judges him** – **the word that I have spoken will judge him**..."*

Speaking about His death Jesus said *concerning any Judgment in the now or in the future **coming from Him or from the Father:***

He said,

John 12:31-33

*"**Now is the Judgment of this world**; now the ruler of this world will be cast out!"*

*"For I, when I am lifted up from the earth, **will draw all Judgment to myself!**"*

*...**past, present, and future!***

*...**once, for all men, for all time!***

*"This He said, to make clear **the kind of death He would die.**"*

And what kind of death did He die?

I mean, yes we know He was lifted up on a cross when He died, *but I do not believe that was the only thing Jesus was referring to.*

What kind of death did He die?

He died **our death!**

He took **our Judgment!**

He took **the punishment that was our due!**

He died once, for all men, for all sin, for all time!

*...**past, present, and future!***

*"For I, when I am lifted up from the earth, **<u>will draw all Judgment to myself</u>!**"*

Isaiah 53:5-11 says it so vividly,

*"He was wounded for **our** transgressions, and He was bruised for **our** iniquities;"*

*"...the chastisement **for our peace** was upon Him,"*

*"... and by His stripes **we are healed**."*

*"...the Lord has laid on Him **the iniquity of us all!**"*

"He was oppressed and He was afflicted,"

"He was led as a lamb to the slaughter,"

"For He was cut off from the land of the living;"

"For the transgression of My people He was stricken"

(He was not just talking about the Jews; *we are all God's people,* amen.

"The earth is the Lord's and the fullness thereof, the world and those that dwell therein" - Psalm 24:1

"Before I formed you in your mother's womb I knew you!" – Jeremiah 1:5. Read also Psalm 139:13-18.)

Isaiah goes on to prophetically speak about Jesus and the work of redemption there in Isaiah 53:

"Yet it pleased the Lord to bruise Him; He has put Him to grief."

*"**But, when You make His soul an offering for sin**, He shall see His seed, He shall prolong His days, and the pleasure of the Lord shall prosper in His hand."*

"Yes, He shall see the travail of His soul and be satisfied!"

Isaiah 40 verse 2 says,

"Speak comfort to Jerusalem,

(…and we know that in the New Testament, the Jerusalem referred to in the Old Covenant, that city of Jerusalem, was just a prophetic picture, pointing to us, people, God's new Jerusalem, God's new dwelling place,

…it refers to that whole work of redemption and what is being communicated to us and to all mankind in that work)

So he says,

"Speak comfort to Jerusalem, and cry out to her, that her warfare is ended, that her iniquity is pardoned; **for she has received from the Lord's hand double for all her sins!"**

In Acts 13:46-47 the apostles **also made it clear**

…that it is not Jesus or the Father who judges you,

…it is you who judge yourself,

…and it is you who bring the inevitable consequences of violating truth upon yourself!

I say again,

Neither the Father, nor Jesus judges anyone, *or will ever judge anyone!*

...because they have already judged everyone!

Over 2014 years ago now Jesus drew all judgment unto Himself,

...past, present and future!

God judged the Son with our transgressions and our iniquities,

...and He died there for us in our place, and so we died there with Him,

...not just so He could free us from all possible judgment from God,

...but so we can be free period!

He died to set us free!

He died to free us from sin; *we died to sin there in Him!*

...and we were raised to newness of life there in Him!

We were justified and glorified there in Him, to enjoy reconciliation with the Father, and righteousness!

We were fully and utterly restored to our sonship there in that work of redemption!

We were fully and utterly restored to our original design there in Him!

"He was put to death because of our sin and was raised because of our justification!"
- Romans 4:25

We were raised to newness of life in Him!

Hallelujah!

"There is therefore now no condemnation to those who are in Christ Jesus!"
– Romans 8:1

"Of God are you in Christ Jesus! He has been made our wisdom from God, our righteousness, our sanctification, and our redemption!" – 1Corinthinas 1:30

Thank you Father!

Thank you Jesus!

There is no more Judgment <u>from God</u> waiting for us!

...but we need to see this clearly!

Jesus could not possibly bear your deliberate violation of truth;

...your deliberate disobedience to the will of God; to the New Covenant!

Jesus could not possibly save you from those consequences;

...Jesus could not possibly save you from that judgment!

...from the inevitable judgment and consequences that come upon you by those things!

I say again, it is like violating the law of gravity!

I don't care if you are a Christian;

...or even if you are the Pope himself,

Ha... ha... ha...

...if you violate gravity, you will go splat!

Listen, if you ignore or violate truth, you remain trapped in darkness; *a slave to the law of sin and death and its wages,*

...and you rob yourself of eternal life.

The apostles said in Acts 13:46-47,

*"**It was necessary** that the Word of God should be declared and revealed to you,"*

"...***but since you reject it, <u>you judge yourself</u> unworthy of eternal life!***"

"Behold, we are now going to the heathen, ***so that they may hear and receive!***"

"For so the Lord has commanded us;

'I have set you to be a light to the Gentiles; ***that you should be that, for salvation to the ends of the earth!***'

Chapter 3

God's concluded His Judgment of us in the Death of Christ!

2Corinthinans 5:9-11 have been so grossly mistranslated in most of our Bible translations that it only adds to our confusion about these things, not that the Greek is messed up, *the Greek is accurate,*

…but the interpretation of the translators is warped by their own law-minded legalistic religious thinking, and leaves much to be desired!

But I love the way my friend Francois du Toit translated that passage.

…In fact I really enjoy the way he translates straight from the Greek and make this passage and its meaning plain in the Mirror Translation.

2Corinthians 5:8-11 from the RSV

"We are of good courage, and we would rather be away from the body and at home with the Lord"

*"So whether we are at home or away, **we make it our aim to please Him.**"*

*"For **we must all appear before the judgment seat of Christ**, so that each one may receive good or evil, according to what he has done in the body."*

"Therefore, knowing the fear of the Lord (the King James Version goes as far as to say: ***"knowing the terror of the Lord"***) ***we persuade men;"***

"…but what we are is known to God, and I hope it is known also to your conscience."

I don't know about you, but the way that reads just left me terrified for many years,

…and it totally messed up our whole concept of evangelism as well!

Now, let me first give you my own version of what Paul just said there, before we read it together out of the Mirror Bible.

Paul says in 2Corinthians 5:9-11 that,

"We make it our aim to be well pleasing to Him, for we now all stand before the judgment seat of Christ, we are faced with that reality, so that each one of us may receive those things we deserve in Him, not based on what we've done in the body, good or bad."

Paul goes on to say there,

"Knowing therefore the fear of the Lord (…or knowing therefore God's love and passion; or having, because of that love, developed our own reverence, our own respect, our own esteem of the Lord and for the Lord; **His passionate love for us is the source of that proper respect and high esteem;**

…Therefore, knowing His love intimately, firsthand), we persuade men"

Proverbs 9:10 says,

"The fear of the Lord (the accurate esteem of who God is) *is the beginning of wisdom,*

(1John 4:8 simply and equivocally declares, **"God is love"**)

Proverbs 9:10 goes on to say,

"…the knowledge of the Holy One is understanding"

But we are not going to go into the whole study of what the fear of the Lord means right now; you can go study it for yourself!

The Mirror Translation goes into so much more detail about 2Corinthins 5:9-11 and I just want to quote it for you here to help you *…because I know that there is lots of people that still* *struggle with this whole idea of Judgment from God;*

…and with the only translations we have had available to us to read, *is it any wonder that they cannot help but wonder whether there isn't going to be perhaps another future Judgment from God,* **even though He already Judged the Son in our stead?**

…but, I like what the Mirror Bible says,

"If we are still to be judged **by God** *for good or bad deeds that we performed in the body,*

…then the judgment that Jesus faced on humanity's behalf would be totally irrelevant!"

Listen, no future judgment could possibly avoid or ignore *the Judgment that already took place in Christ!*

No future event could possibly avoid or ignore *the greatest event of all time and eternity that already took place in the fullness of time;*

…the incarnation and the work of redemption!

I believe there is enough evidence in the Scripture to suggest that *any future Judgment to come will have very little to nothing to do*

with God Judging us, or bringing Judgment upon us,

*...but it will have everything to do **with us and what we bring upon ourselves!***

*It will be our own violation of truth and preferring darkness over light **that will be our judge and bring the experience of its inevitable consequences upon us!***

But, let's read 2Corinthians 5:9-11 from the Mirror Bible now.

5:9 We are totally engaged in the loveliness of that which is of exceedingly great value; whether we are in a physical union with our bodies or a spiritual union with our source; it makes no difference to God's esteem of us! We are highly favored by the Lord. *(The word, **philotimeomai**, comes from **phileo**, meaning dear, fondness; **timay**, meaning value, esteem; and **einai** from **eimi**, I am. The word, **endemeo**, means in union with, entwined; and **ekdemeo** means tied to our source.)*

5:10 For we have all been thoroughly scrutinized in the footsteps of Jesus; *(not as an example for us but of us)* **and are taken care of and restored to the life of our design, regardless of what happened to us in our individual lives, whatever amazing or meaningless things that we encountered in the body.**

*(The word, **phaneroo**, means to render apparent, to openly declare, to manifest. Paul uses the aorist passive infinitive tense **phanerothenai**, not referring to a future event.*

*The aorist tense is **like a snapshot taken of an event that is already concluded.***

*The word, **bematos**, comes from **bayma**, it means footprint, but it is also referring to a raised place mounted by steps, or a tribunal, the official seat of a judge. The word, **komitzo**, comes from **kolumbos**, meaning to tend, to take care of, to provide for, and to carry off from harm.*

*Paul's reference was not how much abuse and affliction he suffered, neither was it the many good times he remembered having, that defined Him; "I am what I am by the grace of God!" If we are still to be judged for good or bad deeds that we performed in the body, **then the judgment that Jesus faced on humanity's behalf seems irrelevant**.)*

5:11 We persuade people in the radiance of the Lord! His visible glory is mirrored in us! Our lives are transparent before God; we anticipate that you will witness the same transparency in your conscience!

*(The word, **suneido**, translates as conscience, **joint seeing**. In 2Corinthians 4:2, "with the open statement of the truth we commend ourselves to everyone's conscience."*

*The word, **phobe**, speaks of dread, terror, and fear! I would prefer to use the word, **<u>phoibe</u>**, which means **radiant!***

*Now that sounds more typical of the God of creation who unveiled Himself in Christ! Jesus is the express image of God, **the radiance of His beauty!** He has made the invisible God visible, and **God is love!***

*…He is the Father of lights with whom there is no shadow due to compromise; **there is no dark side to God!***

To persuade people with fear is in total contradiction to what Paul's ministry was all about!

…not to mention that it is in total contradiction to who God is!

God is love!

See verse 14 of 2Corinthians 5 if you want to really know what Paul's ministry was all about.

Paul says there,

*"…**<u>the love of Christ persuades me</u>** that one has died for all;*

*…this can only mean that **<u>all</u>**, in fact, were equally included in His death!)*

Chapter 4

Much is given!

Let's get back to Luke 12 now.

Verse 48 says,

*"...**every one to whom much is given, of him will much be required**."*

'Now brother Rudi, do you think that that is just? Do you think that God is just to expect that of us?'

Hey you don't have to argue with me over it,

Jesus himself goes on to say,

*"...**every one to whom much is given, of him will much be required, <u>for even to whom men commit much</u> they will demand the more**."*

"To whom much is given, much will be required"

I believe that God is looking for a harvest,

...and God is justified in looking for a harvest!

In Isaiah 53:11 we read that:

"He shall see the fruit of the travail of His soul and be satisfied."

God knows what He has invested on behalf of mankind,

...and therefore He can full well expect a harvest!

When a farmer sows **grade A seed** into the soil,

*...that farmer knows that that grade A seed **definitely has the ability within it to produce a harvest.***

...the farmer knows that about the seed he uses, amen!

He can, therefore, trust that seed.

He can entrust that seed with a commission!

...he can anticipate a sure harvest!

And in the same way **God has made a first class deposit!**

He has made an investment called LIFE into man.

Yes the thief comes, yes the thief deceives, yes he steals, and yes he robs,

...but God has made a significant enough investment of life more abundantly!

It causes us to be more than conquerors!

God is looking for a harvest!

Mark 11:12-13

"On the following day when they came from Bethany, He (Jesus) was hungry,"

"...and seeing in the distance a fig tree in leaf, He went to see if He could find anything on it, but when He came to it He found nothing but leaves."

To me this is a perfect picture of the various religious structures and organizations that are part of our religious system, called *"the Church"* **of today.**

The leaves would make it recognizable as a fig tree,

...in other words it has an outward appearance of godliness, of God's truth and of God's real "Church."

But when God seeks truth,

...when God seeks <u>true fruit</u> on that tree,

...or in that life, or in that church, or in that system,

...He finds only leaves.

Verse 13,

"...*He went to see if He could find anything on it, but when He came to it He found nothing but leaves,* **for it was not the season for figs**."

Now you might reason and say,

'Well, you know, Jesus, you're looking in the wrong season!'

But I believe that what Jesus wants to say to us here *is that He has given us the ability to bear fruit in season and out of season.*

There is a beautiful passage in Ezekiel 47 that prophetically speaks to us,

...about the purpose of God with His revelation of truth;

...about the purpose of God with **the revelation of the successful redemption of man, in Christ Jesus**, *which He has entrusted to His Church!*

He speaks of us being trees, *the planting of the Lord,*

He describes us as *beautiful fruit bearing trees,*

*...planted securely with our roots drawing from the river of life, **bearing fruit continuously, in season and out of season!***

Let's read it!

Ezekiel 47:12

"And on the banks, on both sides of the river, there will grow all kinds of trees for food, their leaves will not wilt, nor their fruit fail, but they will bear fresh fruit <u>every month</u>,"

"...because the water for them flows from the sanctuary."

That's their secret!

And if that water flows from the sanctuary,

*...then God is expecting in our lives **a constant production of life and fruit.** Amen!*

In Mark, chapter 12 verse 1 & 2

"He began to speak to them in parables,

*'A man planted a vineyard, and set a hedge around it, and dug a pit for the wine press, and built a tower **and then let it out to tenants and went into another country**...'*

So, this man **had a vision,**

...and he prepared the ground and made preparations **to accommodate that vision.**

This man had a sure goal in his heart!

He knew what could be produced through this vineyard!

He wanted a harvest!

...so he did all the necessary groundwork to prepare for the harvest,

...and after he was done,

...his vineyard **had everything necessary to accommodate that vision** *for a harvest!*

So, after setting it all up and setting the stage for the harvest,

...*he then entrusted a stewardship to a certain group of people.*

Verse 2,

"*...and when the time came he sent a servant to the tenants to get some of the fruit of the vineyard.*"

God is looking for a harvest!

God wants to eat some of the fruit of His investment in our lives!

"...he sent a servant to the tenants to get some of the fruit of the vineyard, but they took him and beat him up..."

...and we know the rest of the story!

Verse 9 says,

"What will the owner of the vineyard do? He will come and destroy those wicked tenants and give the vineyard to others."

...he will give the vineyard to others!

From the Jews *to the Church!*

...from those who thought they had a claim upon it,

...to those who had no claim at all!

...from so-called leadership,

...to regular, genuine, down to earth, real people!

...from the religious system, *to the unmarried women!*

...from the un-faithful,

...to the faith-full!

...from the disobedient,

...to the obedient!

...from the supposed some-bodies, to the nobodies!

Isaiah 54:1 says so clearly,

"Sing o barren one, you who did not bear, for the children of the desolate will be more than the children of the married woman."

If those who are married to the religious system are *not producing the real harvest*,

...then God will give His vineyard to others,

...because God is expecting a real harvest from His investment in this world!

If you sowed your son, *would you expect a so-so, poor excuse for a harvest?*

The best that the religious system of today can produce is a bunch of weak and feeble babies that does not even remotely resemble the image of a son God has in mind!

God wants mature sons that fully understand redemption truth and fully resemble the image and likeness of Jesus!

...fruit-bearing sons!

...strong in love and revelation and therefore capable!

...well able to bring in *the kind of harvest God expects from His investment!*

Isaiah 55:10 & 11 says,

"As the rain and the snow comes down from heaven and return not thither, but water the earth, making it bring forth and sprout, giving seed to the sower and bread to the eater, ***so shall My Word be that goes forth from My mouth!***

*"It shall not return to Me empty but **it shall accomplish <u>that which I purpose</u>***

...and prosper <u>in the thing for which I sent it</u>.*"*

There is potential in that seed to prosper and to produce *after its own kind!*

...after the exact and accurate purpose of God!

In 2Peter 1:1 Peter says,

"I am writing to those who have obtained <u>a faith of equal standing</u> with ours,"

*"...**in the righteousness of our God and Savior Jesus Christ*** (...in His perfect work of redemption!)*"*

The audience here is people, *any people,*

...and His subject is the perfect work of redemption,

...and we were all included in that!

...so He is speaking to us as well!

Why can we be so bold to make such a claim?

For in the Scriptures,

...in the knowledge of God,

...we have all obtained a faith of equal standing,

...and, therefore, of equal potential!

...equal potential to that of the apostle's faith,

...and of Jesus' faith,

...and of the faith of God!

And then Peter says in verse 8,

"If these things are in you and abound,

...they will keep you from being ineffective,

*...**or barren, or unfruitful, in the knowledge of our Lord Jesus Christ***"

...in the understanding of the incarnation,

...he is referring to the understanding of the truth revealed in our Lord Jesus Christ!

...and to the understanding of redemption realities brought about in Him; in His death, burial, and resurrection!

Chapter 5

Sing O Barren One!

God doesn't want any one of us, *barren or unfruitful!*

Isaiah 54:1 says,

"Sing o barren one, enlarge the place of your tent!"

Maybe your religious experience has been that of a barren women for many years now already;

…You've never led somebody to the Lord and enlightened them to the truth of redemption,

…or you use to lead people to the Lord and to the truth, when you first got saved, *but that has now been many years ago.*

…You've never really seen God work a real miracle in someone else's life through your life,

…or He used to, *but not lately.*

…You've never really had answers to your prayers, or you used to, *but not anymore.*

And by now you have been accommodating that statuesque *for so long in your life*,

...that you have come to think that that is all that religion is all about!

Listen; there is more to Christianity than just paying your tithes, and coming to church, and praying and reading your Bible!

True Christianity is not bachelor-flat living; you know, *just you and your own needs and you've become very comfortable with your situation.*

But now the voice of God and the Word of God comes to challenge you right here in this book!

Ha... ha... ha...

And He says to you,

"Sing o barren one!"

'Why should *I* sing? For, *I* can't do anything for God man!'

Listen, God's Word of truth wants to conceive fruit in your life!

God wants us to become fruitful through His revelation knowledge,

...and expand our capacity, *so we can enlarge the place of our tent*,

...so that we can be able to bring in and accommodate *the kind of quality harvest He desires!*

My confidence is in the Word of God, *and in its ability within you,*

...not in your ability to crank up something for the Lord!

I know that the enemy would seek to oppose God's truth!

I know that he would seek to oppose you!

I know that he would seek to frustrate your life,

...so you feel,

'Well, I'm not sure if this is going to work for me.'

But listen, there is something I know about you, about all believers, I know that,

"Greater is He that is at work in you than he that is in the world."

I know that,

"We overcome the evil one by the word of our testimony."

I know that this Word;

...God's truth concerning you and concerning your redemption in Christ Jesus,

...will inevitably produce a testimony!

It will produce its harvest in you!

...and it will produce its harvest through you!

Because God says His Word will not return to Him empty handed!

Chapter 6

God's image and inscription

Let's turn to the book of Mark in your Bible quickly,

I want to show you something,

They asked Jesus a question and He responded, *but not in a way they expected,*

Mark 12:15-17

"'Should we pay tribute to Caesar or not?'

"But knowing their hypocrisy he said to them,

'Why put me to the test?'

'Bring me a coin and let me look at it,'

"…and they brought Him one, and He said to them,

'Whose likeness and inscription is this?'

They said to Him,

'Caesar's'

"...and He said,

*'Render then unto Caesar the things that belong to Caesar **and unto God the things that belong to God.'"***

When I pondered on that *I began to see something* in this parable Jesus used;

...something He really wanted us to grasp!

He said,

'Bring Me a coin. Whose inscription, whose investment is this?'

...and while I was reading that I heard God's voice in my spirit,

...as if Jesus were really saying,

*'Bring me a man. **Whose likeness is in that man!***

Whose inscription!

Whose life deposit is in that man!

Whose investment is in that man?'

'Should we pay tribute to God or not?'

'Should we highly esteem and reverence God or not?'

'Render then to God what belongs to God,

...for you too are created in the image and likeness of God!'

We have potential within each and every one of us *to become bearers of His image,*

...to reflect and to exhibit the brightness of His likeness and His glory!

And people all over America, and all over the world, and even in the Church, *somehow ironically thinks that,*

...success in life means to have a fat bank account!

Praise God if that fat bank account is there *to be used in going forth to make known the Gospel,*

...but if that fat bank account is the image of your life,

...then you're a poor man!

Because God created me to be a bearer of His image; *not an image of our own making!*

*...*listen, richness is not measured by how many images I can collect of George Washington, Andrew Jackson, or Benjamin Franklin for that matter,

...but true riches are measured by how much of the image of the Creator God can be reflected and exhibited,

...and be on display in my life!

That's the true riches that the scriptures speak of.

The true riches is me becoming an image bearer of Christ!

...so that the brightness of His glory and of His beauty

...and the true value of what He has given us can shine forth from us!

If there is value in money to purchase something,

...then there is imperishably more value;

...there is value of infinite proportions <u>to that treasure of the image of Christ</u> that God has made me a steward of and wants me to render unto Him!

"*...render therefore unto Caesar what belongs to Caesar,*

...but render unto God what belongs to God!"

Chapter 7

Be a good steward!!

"Render then unto Caesar the things that belong to Caesar,

...and render unto God the things that belong to God!"

That word *"render"* means **to be a steward of**

Having that money means you are a steward of the things that belong to Caesar, *or the US government and the American People.*

It means that you serve Caesar in the things that belong to Caesar;

...you serve the American People in the things that belong to the American People and the US Government *that is supposed to represent them.*

In other words, Caesar or the US government, or the American people, through the US government, *entrusted you to be a good steward of the things that belong to him or to them.*

"...but render unto God the things that belong to God!"

Jesus said,

"...let your light so shine before man!"

Let's go to Luke 19:12-15

"A nobleman went into a far country to receive a kingdom and then to return."

"Calling ten of his servants, he gave them ten pounds, and he said to them,"

'Trade with these till I come'

That word *"Trade"* would suggest:

Do business with what I've given you.

Do business until I come.

Mean business with what I've given you!

Don't just put it somewhere *where it's just going to gather dust,*

But begin to use it to purchase and increase, amen.

In verse 15 we read,

"But when he returned, having received the kingdom, he commanded these servants to

whom he had given the money to be called to him, **that he might know what they had gained by their trading**"

I want you to know that just as surely as you are reading this book today;

…there is coming a day, **and now is,** *that God is calling every one of us, your wife, your husband, even your children, to account,*

…because He is excited over His investment in us, and He wants to know what we have gained by our trading with it!

*…***even now,** *not just at the end of this life,* **even now,** *God is calling us into account!*

…He has given us heavenly currency, truth, a treasure of eternal infinite worth and value in our spirits,

…and He is excited to see what we will gain in our hearts from what He has given us!

…He is excited to discover and to see and to know what we have truly gained by our trading with it!

I believe that one day at the end of our lives, at the end of this life, we will not be called into account *on the sins we've committed,*

...because Jesus was wounded for our transgressions, He was bruised for our iniquities,

BUT I am fully persuaded that one day we will all, every believer will, we will all stand face to face before our Father and before our God,

*...**and in that day I will not be ashamed to stand there,***

*...**because every bit of fruit, every crown of glory, it all comes from Him,***

*...**from His working within me both to will and to do of His good pleasure!***

*...**I will lay that proverbial crown at His feet,***

*...**and we will enjoy that fruit together,***

*...**and celebrate together what His seed, what His word of truth by revelation produced in me and through me!***

There will be no room for boasting in His presence, **only rejoicing with Him,**

...because,

"What do we have that we did not receive from Him, and by His working within us both to will and to do of His good pleasure?"

...and you see, our yielding to it comes easy,

"...we love Him <u>because He first loved us</u>!"

Luke 19:15

*"But when he returned, having received the kingdom, he commanded these servants to whom he had given the money to be called to him, **that he might know what they had gained by their trading**"*

...what they had gained from the truth of redemption and by sharing that truth!

...that He might see and know and rejoice in what we have done with what He has entrusted us with!

...for He has entrusted us with revelation truth that contain a commission!

Oh, what a day of rejoicing that will be for us who believe!

...because we have yielded to His Spirit of Truth and to that Word of truth; that word of redemption and reconciliation,

...that revelation He comes to show us and plant into our spirit,

...that it may bear fruit in our heart and in our life!

He has entrusted us with a commission *to take what we know,*

…to take what we receive in Him,

…and to trade with it,

…in our spirit in the first place,

…and also in our lives,

…and in our relationships and conversations with others,

…and thus to develop its full potential!

You see, in that *"pound"* **there is a potential!**

When I entrust you with a pound, *I entrust you with a potential,*

…and if you are trust-worthy,

…if you are a steward of that pound,

…listen, you didn't work for that pound,

…you've just been shown trust, that's it, that's all,

…and so you are given that pound,

…and you can see in that pound that is in your hand *…a potential harvest,*

...that potential is immediately linked to it!

...It is linked to the pound in your hand!

...it is linked to what God has deposited, through truth, in your very spirit!

God wants to quicken that eye of faith within our hearts, *to see that potential!*

...to see the pound for what it's worth!

...to see that I've been shown trust,

...and to count it as a great privilege and an honor!

...to fully recognize my stewardship of it,

...so that its potential would not be lost!

...so that God's grace would not be wasted on me!

...so that the potential of that pound would not be wasted in being entrusted to me!

...so that its harvest would not be lost!

...so that that harvest through me would not be lost by me!

Whenever we come together, when we gather as a group, or meet one on one, or fellowship together, even in this book you are reading, God wants us to see more than just another meeting, than just a religious Sunday morning service, than just a religious meeting!

...than just another religious book we can pick up and easily forget again!

He wants us to see more than just another teaching!

He wants us to see that it's a pound that He entrusts me with!

There is infinite eternal value in that Word!

...in that redemption truth!

God wants us to see that that Word that comes out of His mouth,

...that authentic original Word revealed and restored to us in Christ,

...concerning out true identity,

...concerning the restoration of our original design,

...the restoration of His image and likeness in us,

...the restoration of our sonship,

...in His work of redemption,

...that revelation has the potential to give seed to the sower,

...and bread for food,

...and to multiply,

...into a harvest of righteousness!

If we begin to have that attitude,

...and say,

'Father God, every Word that you entrust me with, I'm going to begin to change my attitude towards it!'

'*...so I can see the full potential in that Word,*'

'*...so that I can put it to work,*'

'*...and see the increase, and the fruit,*'

'*...that inevitably comes from that Word!*'

Not one of us has the right to sit back and be entertained by the ministry of the Word!

...because God says,

"To whom much is given, much is required,"

...**not by your pastor, not by your husband, not by your wife, not by your parents, not by me,**

...*but by God Himself*

...*who entrusts us* **with that precious truth and that beautiful revelation of our salvation** *and of all men's salvation also,* **in that redemption work of Jesus.**

"Render to God the things that belong to God!"

Chapter 8

Necessity is laid upon us!

That's why Paul says in 1Corinthians 9:16

"Woe to me if I preach not the gospel,"

He says,

"…necessity is laid upon me"

Romans 1:14,

He says,

"I am under obligation, both to the Jews and the Gentiles,"

"…to preach the Gospel!"

"I owe them what I know!"

"I owe them the Gospel!"

"Jesus did what He did, for them, not just for me!"

He says in 2Corinthinas 5:14,

"I have come to a conclusion in the Gospel!"

"Not so that I may now become sentimental and religious and legalistic and dogmatic about it!"

"But the love of Christ constrains me!"

"That truth of His love has become a compelling influence within me"

"That love of Christ is a driving force in my life!"

"Because I have thus concluded …I have seen it clearly!"

"This is what I've seen!"

"This is what the love of Christ constrains me to see!"

"If one died for all, <u>then all died</u>!"

"They are included!"

"…and now I owe it to the world to tell them the good news!"

"…to enlighten them!"

"…to tell them what God has done for them!"

"…to tell them that <u>they are free</u>!"

…and they can be free <u>now</u>;

...they don't have to wait, amen!

They can be free!

Paul says in verse 16,

"Listen, that love is working in me to such a degree that I can no longer see any man from a human point of view,

...according to their natural man;

...according to their achievements or their natural identity, or even their weaknesses and their failures and their sins!"

"All I want to do is awaken them <u>to their true identity</u> as sons of God!"

"All I want to do is awaken them <u>to their true design restored to them already</u> in Christ's work of redemption!"

"All I want to do is awaken them to the fact that they are free already!"

"...free from all their sins and the weaknesses and their failures and their restrictive natural identity, even their so-called achievements and successes and reasons for pride in their life!"

"They are free already!"

"Free from all that junk!"

"Totally totally free!"

"...and all I want to do is awaken them to that!"

"Awaken them!"

"All I want to do is point them to that truth!"

"...to the truth of who they really really are!"

"Children of God!"

"...and their Daddy loves them!"

"He is in love with them!"

"All I want to do is awaken them and point them to that image and likeness of God within them,"

"...which they have been restored to in the work of redemption and can now give full expression to"

"All they have to do is clearly see and embrace fully that work of redemption,"

"...and that love of Christ!"

"...to this end I then also labor," he says,

"...in fact I labor more than any of my companions in the Gospel,"

"...with a zeal that is from God!"

"...yet it's not I, it's that grace of God that is with me,"

"...it's that love of God that is burning here in my heart!"

"It is God Himself who is my constant companion!"

"...and that revelation God and I share together here in my bosom, here in my heart, here in my spirit, is the very thing that is producing the fruit that is coming out of my life!"

"God is producing His own harvest!"

"God's truth, God's faith, God's own conclusion in the Gospel is bringing forth and bringing in its own harvest!"

"...and supplying the energy to do it!"

Hallelujah!

"I am not merely relying on my own zeal; my own dogmatic religious legalistic zeal!"

"The energy and source where this fruit and this harvest comes from is not my own energy, my own religious zeal for God ...an ignorant zeal not according to knowledge!"

"No! I am relying on the knowledge and the revelation of God <u>I treasure here within me</u>!"

"...It produces its own energy!"

"...its own zeal!"

"...not a zeal <u>for</u> God,"

"...but the very zeal <u>of</u> God!"

"...not by my own works!"

"Listen, I have nothing to boast about!"

"It is that revelation of God; that revelation of redemption <u>I cherish within my spirit</u> that produces it all!"

Jesus says in Matthew 10:27

"What you've heard in private, <u>proclaim</u> upon the housetops."

It means you cannot afford to keep any revelation to yourself!

If you keep any revelation to yourself *it will rot!*

If you keep any revelation to yourself and think,

'Well, you know, ***I've discovered the secret of God's divine embrace and God's healing***

power, *or whatever,* ***and I'm just going to keep it to myself and my family.'***

I'm telling you *it will rot!*

…it will stop working for you soon after you received it and didn't share it,

…or it may keep working for you, **but it brings leanness to your soul!**

*But God wants us to **receive** revelation from Him,*

…and have the attitude,

*'God I'm going to take this **and get on a housetop somewhere**,'*

*'I'm going to take this **and proclaim it to my neighborhood and to the whole world!'***

Housetop ministry means neighborhood ministry!

Ha… ha… ha…

It means impacting the world!

I'm going to let my neighbor know,

…even my neighbor over there in another country,

…because I see they're suffering,

Listen, they're on the verge of a divorce, they're suffering financially, and they're suffering this and that and the other thing, at the hands of the devil, *because of their ignorance,*

...they're suffering needlessly!

...and I know that I've discovered something to communicate with them!

I can tell them that,

'Listen man, this Bible is more than an old fat book full of rules and regulations;'

<u>*'God's life is invested in this Word!'*</u>

'...and this Word has come forth from His mouth, <u>and His Word cannot return to Him void</u>.'

So, I'm going to talk to my family members, even my extended family I haven't seen in a while and don't know so well,

...and I'm going to knock even on my neighbor's door!

...and I'm going to go to them,

...I'm going to go to the nations!

I know the guy might be annoyed because I am so bold and rude to come into his space *and invade his privacy,*

But I'm going to say,

'Sir, I've got a Word for you from God, and I've also got a word of truth for you, redemption truth, gospel truth,

…good news, not bad news,'

'…and I know this Word works, because it works for me and my wife and my family.'

And what I'm sharing with him is not just religious nonsense;

…it's not a lying word on how to escape the wrath of God!

…it's not a word on how to escape hell and make it into heaven!

…some cheap grace fire insurance!

…and it's not just some futuristic word either,

…some word that has no bearing on life in the here and now!

…it's not just a word about some golden daybreak of going to Heaven someday!

'No, but If you grasp this, sir, yes, you are going to go to Heaven someday,

...<u>but it's a word that I can put to practice in my daily encounter with life</u>!'

Hey listen, God wants to put <u>that kind of confidence</u> in us!

God wants to put,

...<u>by</u> His truth and <u>by</u> His Spirit, and <u>by</u> the anointing that comes from Him, <u>by</u> His love,

...God wants to put that kind of confidence in us ...because He holds us responsible for that!

In 2Timothy 1:7 Paul declares that,

"God has not given us a spirit of timidity and fear, but He has given unto us a strong dynamic vibrant spirit, full of life, full of a love for life!

He has given us a dynamic bold spirit, full of love, and full of the power of God.

We have a sound mind, because He has made it sound by His love and by His truth!"

...and we are therefore able to love people, and to gently reason with them in the truth, and to persuade them of the love of God ...to minister to them by the power of God!

Chapter 9

Boldness & Confidence!

Now, **if I entrusted some confidence in you**,

…say I'm a big company manager and I am looking for some salesmen,

…and I gave you a certain area and I say,

'All right, I'm entrusting that area to you,'

'…and here's how you're going to do it,'

'…and I give you the recipe'

'…and I give you the tools to go and do it,

Then obviously I put my confidence in you and I feel like I could trust in you!

And I know that I have given you everything necessary to get the job done!

…and therefore, *I'd realize that you could actually take what you've got, spiritually speaking as well,*

…*and begin to work with that,*

...and begin to influence that neighborhood or that region,

...or the whole country and the world for that matter!

Listen, if you're a salesmen,

...you're going to have to walk into situations where you are going to face all kinds of people,

...but you're motivated to face them!

You're motivated to face them!

You're not embarrassed and feeling,

'Well you know, I've got this product, but it's not really going to help you, you know, actually that other company's product is much better ...and ...'

Hey listen, *that kind of opinion, that mentality, that thinking, that attitude will never get the job done!*

You're going to have to be *convinced* **that you are offering a product <u>of extreme worth and of the utmost value</u> to your neighbor!**

...before you can even dream of being that good salesmen!

And let me tell you, we are not peddling the Word of God!

We don't have to try and sell nothing!

God's truth is of infinitely more value *than any product you can ever show up with at any man's door!*

Those worldly sales people and those religious sales people are motivated by a paycheck, *or by deception, by their own religious zeal, or by fear,*

…but they don't really really care about the person on the other side of that door!

…it's more about them than it is about that other person!

But now we come in love, *and we do care!*

…and we forget about ourselves,

…and love for our neighbor compels us,

…God's love for them, and our love for them too, because of the gospel, because of the working of God within us,

…that love compels us and motivates us!

…and we're not there trying to sell them anything!

...no, we have the greatest news to share that is of the utmost importance to their lives!

...absolutely pertinent to everything about them and to who they really are!

And what we have to share is of the greatest value!

What we have to share *is love!*

Real love!

What we have to share *is truth!*

Genuine truth!

The truth of the love of God!

The truth of His love for them!

And of our love for them also,

...because of what we know to be true about them in Christ Jesus!

...because we see them as family!

...we love them!

...and what we have to give them is Love Himself,

...it is genuine friendship with Him and with us,

...nothing fake!

What we have to share with them and impart to them and give them *is of real worth, practical worth!*

And I believe that so often the enemy keeps us *so ignorant,*

...so blinded and dull of hearing,

...that we don't even realize the value of God's investment, not even as far as our own lives are concerned,

...never mind our neighbors' lives!

When that Samaritan woman came to drink from that well, from that water,

...we read about that in that, account John gave about her, in John chapter four,

Jesus said to her,

"Hey lady, I'll give you a drink of <u>My water</u>, the water I personally partake of, and when you drink of <u>this water I have to offer</u>,

...it will become within you a fountain of living water."

Now a fountain is a neighborhood ministry!

Ha... ha... ha...

It's a ministry to your neighbor!

Whether it's your neighbor next door,

...or the stranger and the foreigner there at Wall-Mart,

...or your neighbor that lives in another part of the world, amen!

Hallelujah!

A fountain is not just for me and my wife and my children and my family!

Man I cannot stop that fountain because it gushes forth!

Jesus said it will become rivers of living water, gushing forth out of your innermost being!

You cannot stop a fountain!

...especially a gusher the size of 'Old Faithful!'

You cannot stop that fountain of God within you from flowing!

You cannot stop an artesian well from flowing!

You cannot stop a river from flowing, never mind *rivers!*

How can you keep that kind of artesian fountain *within your piece of property?*

How can you keep a river on your piece of property?

...never mind rivers?

That fountain and those rivers are just going to flow out *and break past the boundary of your property,*

...and continue on into your neighbor's property and beyond!

...it is meant to flow all the way to the ocean!

...all the way to the nations!

Jesus says,

"I'm going to give you a fountain; I'm going to give you rivers of living water, life-giving water; I'm going to give you <u>a ministry</u>."

Chapter 10

Take your place!

Listen, *every believer has received a faith of equal standing,*

...*within the truth of the love of God; within the truth of the gospel we have heard, we have all received *a faith of equal standing,

...a faith of equal ability,

...a faith of equal potential!

God wants us to discover that *I have a potential invested in me,*

...that God has shown trust in my life!

And God wants to develop that potential in me,

***...*through His Word; through His redemption truth, and through His Spirit, and through His love,**

...*so that I can become a blessing to my neighborhood, *and to the nations,

...so I can be the salt of the earth!

So that when the enemy comes in, *like a flood of truth coming out of me; like a flood of strong faith, God can raise up a standard against him through my life!*

I don't need to be overwhelmed by the evil of this world!

In the midst of this troubled economic time,

...and troubled political time,

...and whatever trouble there may be,

...I can <u>stand</u> under His reign of righteousness,

...under the reign of His peace and prosperity and blessing!

Praise God!

God wants to prosper and bless us in our spirit with abundance of living that spill over in our life, and makes every difference in our lives, and through our lives!

Listen, abundant living has nothing to do with the size of your bank account or the amount of your possessions!

The truth is; our treasure is in the fact that we've obtained pure love and truth, and with it therefore a faith of equal standing!

Mathew 10:25

"It is enough for a disciple to be like his teacher."

You see the disciples had the same mentality as the Church today.

They thought,

'Well, as long as we have Jesus around,

...He's going to get the job done quickly,'

'As long as we have the evangelist or the revivalist or the great apostle or prophet or whomever he may be,

...he's going to get the job done for us!'

'...and we're just going to stand back and enjoy His powerful preaching and teaching and ministry.'

No!

Jesus says,

"A disciple <u>is like his teacher</u>"

That means, *entrusted with the same commission,*

...with the same authority ...and therefore with that same responsibility!

1John 4:17 says,

"As He is so are we in this world!"

Jesus says,

"I give unto <u>you</u> the keys of the kingdom,

...so that whatever is legally bound in heaven, because of your covenant, because of that work of redemption, <u>you</u> may bind on earth;

...whatever is already having been loosed in heaven, <u>you</u> may loose on earth!"

So that means *I can stand in His responsibility here on earth to do His will!*

Listen, the power is in the integrity of God's Word!

...it's not in the way pastor Rudi or pastor so-and-so says it, just so, in a particular way.

'It just sounds so much more affective when <u>you</u> say it, pastor Rudi!'

Ha... ha... ha...

No don't be deceived!

The power is in the integrity of God's Word!

The power is in the truth of His Word!

The power is in His word, in the message, in His tremendous, unending, unfailing love; the power is in the Gospel!

"The gospel is the power of God!"

You might go and witness to somebody and it comes out all jumbled and shaky *and just plain messed up,*

…but you just watch and see your God perform those miracles!

*Listen as **you** speak forth God's Word,*

*…**you shall be** as God's mouth!*

It shall be as if Jesus is ministering through you!

Because God confirms His Word!

It's His gospel, it's His love we're sharing not our own.

Amen!

It's His Spirit we rely on; it's Him, amen!

We don't rely on ourselves!

It's a love thing from beginning to end!

It's a Spirit thing from beginning to end!

It's a faith thing, from beginning to end, amen!

It's a faith thing!

It's a love thing!

It's a heart thing!

…and God is watching over His Word to perform it!

…whether we ourselves feel good about it or not,

…whether we feel sick,

…whether we even feel good or not,

*…**whether we feel anointed or not!***

God is watching over His Word to perform it!

I thank God **His love is His love, *and it has an impact!***

I thank God **His Word is His Word!**

*…yesterday, tomorrow, today, **any day!***

His Word is His Word!

His Word doesn't change!

His love doesn't change!

He doesn't change, amen!

He is unchanging!

God is always in a good mood!

He is always ready to perform His Word!

He is always ready to minister to people!

...because God has been in love with mankind from before time began!

Again, a salesman has confidence in the product he offers, *and not so much in his own personality.*

What we have to offer, is a product of worth, *of eternal worth, and of infinite value!*

...and that's what gives us guts,

...that's what gives us confidence,

...to proclaim His love, to proclaim His gospel message!

...with a conviction and an anointing!

Proverbs 8:1-3

"Does not wisdom call?

(Now remember 1Corinthians 1 says that, *"He (Jesus) was been made unto us wisdom"* so,)

*"...does not wisdom **call**, does not understanding **raise her voice**?"*

When would someone raise their voice?

Obviously, *when they have something to say!*

*"She takes her stand **on the hill** beside the highway"*

That's the highway leading right into your town

Ha... ha... ha...

"Yes even in the path she takes her stand."

*"...beside the gate, right in front of the town. At the entrance of the portal **she cries aloud**."*

Why?

Because she's got something to say!

She's got something worth saying!

So, she takes her product and makes it available in the market place where people are at!

It's no use to go and preach to the trees or on a busy corner somewhere *because at least you were seen doing something weird.*

It's no use trying to go and preach downtown during rush-hour, or on a busy corner, where nobody is even listening to you, *because nobody even have the time to stop and chat,*

No one was listening, man, so stop bragging about what you did!

...and think you earned some kind of badge of honor that now makes you super spiritual!

...but at least you preached it!

Ha... ha... ha...

Listen, doing something weird *doesn't make you spiritual!*

...*or somehow more mature than the next guy!*

Verse 5 says,

"Oh simple ones, learn prudence, oh foolish men, pay attention."

Hey, that doesn't just apply to the ones we're trying to reach and share with.

It does, amen, *but it applies to us, as well!*

Stop doing religious things that don't work, *just so you can say you did it!*

And stop doing religious things that make you look weird! *It doesn't work!*

If what you are doing doesn't work, *use wisdom and try something else!*

Genuinely connecting with people,

...actually reaching them is all that matters!

...not so you can get a prayer out of them and put another feather into your cap,

...but nothing really changes!

I'm talking about making a genuine connection with people,

...a real connection, heart to heart in spirit dimension, in the spirit realm, and sharing redemption truth with them, the truth of the gospel, the good news,

...so that they can fall in love with God and begin to genuinely live life with Him and for Him who died for them!

Do what works!

Make a real heart and spirit connection with individual people!

Even when speaking to whole crowds, *Jesus never overlooked the individual!*

In fact whenever He spoke to a crowd *He always addressed the individual,*

…just like I am doing in this book with you!

Avoid generalizations!

Speak to people, *not past them!*

Make it real and personal!

Nothing else works!

Stop condemning them, **and share the <u>good news</u> with them!**

Share the love of God with them!

Share with them their value before God; their true value to God, their worth!

Share with them how He sees them, how much He loves them, who they are in His eyes, demonstrated by the price He was willing to pay, just to prove it!

Strike up a friendly conversation *till you see that they are open to hear what you have to say,*

...and then start steering the conversation in the direction of the gospel!

Don't argue over truth!

Speak the truth *in love!*

In other words, *love is the truth that goes beyond all truth!*

Make known His love!

Let love speak!

Let LOVE HIMSELF speak!

God's redemption of man in Christ is not just about truth!

It is all about love!

I say again,

LET LOVE SPEAK!

Chapter 11

The content of our message!

Romans 10:14 says,

(…and I paraphrase again,)

"How then shall they be able to believe if they have not heard?"

"How then shall they be able to relate to us and our message, or connect with Him in whom they have not believed, because we did not present it in wisdom and we did not present it accurately and we did not present it in genuine love?"

"How shall they hear, without a messenger to serve them, by sharing with them the accurate message?"

…by sharing with them the deep deep genuine love of God?"

Proverbs 8:5 says,

"Hear for I will speak noble things and from my lips will come what is right and true."

…I will reveal the truth, in love, to you!

Verse 18,

"**True** riches and honor are with me, **enduring** wealth and prosperity."

Verse 19,

"My fruit **is better** than gold, even fine gold, and my yield than choice silver."

Now don't you think this Gospel; the true Gospel of man's deliverance in Christ, and of God's love and acceptance and embrace and reconciliation is a message that the world *would <u>want to</u> hear?*

"**True** riches and honor are with me, **enduring** wealth and prosperity."

"My fruit **is better** than gold, even fine gold, and my yield than choice silver."

Don't you think this is a message that the world *would <u>want</u> to hear,*

...because they don't know anything about enduring wealth!

All they've come to know is *temporary wealth,*

...even in religion,

...even in the Christian religion,

...because the Christian religion, and religion in general, is full of this teaching and that teaching and empty dogmatic legalistic rituals and doctrines,

...but it has very little truth, amen!

...very little real love and truth of any lasting value and wealth!

All that people have come to know in the world is temporary wealth!

One day they've got everything *and tomorrow it's gone,*

...and all the world has come to know in religion is *temporary wealth!*

One day they've got everything, *but tomorrow it's gone!*

But I thank God for redemption realities!

I thank God for true Christianity!

I thank God for the love of God!

I thank God for Jesus!

I thank God that enduring wealth has a root system!

...and it's related to <u>seeking first</u> <u>His</u> kingdom <u>within you</u>!

…and the revelation of righteousness!

…it's related to the truth of the gospel!

…to the work of redemption!

…and living in the abundance of that reconciled love relationship with Jesus!

Proverbs 8:19 says,

*"My fruit **is better** than gold, even fine gold, and my **yield** than choice silver."*

Did you get that?

Wisdom produces a harvest!

If I begin to encounter wisdom *and I give ear and incline my heart to hear what wisdom says to me,*

…listen, through the knowledge of Jesus;

…through the love of God for me revealed there,

…through the revelation of redemption, all things have been granted to me that pertain to life and Godliness!

Now, if I begin to encounter this wisdom, this love, and I begin to give ear and incline my heart to hear what wisdom says to me,

...and if therefore these things are in me and abound,

...then <u>they</u> will keep me from being barren and unfruitful!

<u>They</u> will keep me from just living an isolated life,

...and 'I am so alone, no one wants to come and visit me, no one wants to be around me and I'm not worth anything'

I am telling you now; *this gospel and this revelation I am sharing with you today <u>is the end of loneliness</u>!*

You'll never ever again have a dull life *if you start living this way!*

We've got to promote the knowledge of Jesus.

We've got to promote His love!

We've got to promote the value and the worth by which He values everyone!

We have got to present the fruit of the spirit in our lives to people.

We've got to give them a taste of the living God, and of His love, and of what He is doing in our lives through His redemption truth.

We cannot expect the area we live in, or this nation, or this world, *to just change their attitude towards God,*

…we cannot just think,

'Well the churches are doing their job.'

Listen, God's not holding those church buildings responsible *for drawing people into His kingdom!*

…into His love.

…into the kingdom of the son of His love!

He's holding us the people responsible,

We are the church, not those church buildings!

He has entrusted us with *a sure Word.*

The Word of God is guaranteed.

The truth of the gospel *will work!*

His love works!

…if we just represent it and communicate it accurately!

Chapter 12

Fully embrace God's Word in your heart!

When I give you a seed, *you can take that seed and eat it.*

That's what I'm doing here in this book,

...or when you meet together with your fellow believers, there where you live, *take the seed and eat it.*

In this book, and when we meet together, *we are supposed to take that Word and that love, and receive it and embrace it,*

...and that's what we're living on,

...and wow, it's so delicious, and we enjoy it for ourselves.

But hey listen; *you shouldn't live on Sunday morning's messages,*

...or on the nuggets of truth and love you get from this book!

You should go and get your own manna every morning and eat the truth of the Word of God for yourself!

Your Bible and this book are not bread; *it is seed!*

Listen my ministry from the pulpit, and my ministry one on one, or my ministry of book-writing *is not a bread ministry.*

I'm not feeding the homeless here!

I'm putting seed in your heart *so you can go and take this seed and plant it*

...and go and reap a crop from it for yourself!

Go and reap a harvest *to feed all your friends and your whole neighborhood, amen!*

So often we think,

'Well I'm going to Sunday morning service, and I'm going to get a nice little short message and there I sit.'

But see, while you have that mentality *that message will never have its full impact in your life,*

...because you think,

'I'm just here for my needs, I'm just going to get my needs met this morning.'

Listen God's going to get your needs met *in any case,*

...but if that's all you've come for you've wasted your time, and God's time!

You need to say in your heart,

'God I'm here as a responsible person, I'm committed to the enlargement and extension of Your kingdom. I'm dedicated to the full impact of Your Word and of Your love upon this earth. I'm committed, o God, to be a faithful steward of Your grace.'

Peter says in 1Peter 4:10

"We must be faithful stewards of God's manifold Grace; of His inexhaustible multidimensional love, employing our gifts to bless one another."

Proverbs 8:34 says,

*"**Happy** is the man, who listens to me."*

That's where happiness comes from,

...a relationship with the Word,

...a relationship with the wisdom of the truth of redemption!

...a relationship with the love of God,

...with the God who is love!

*"Happy is the man, who listens to me, watching **daily** at my gates."*

(...now-and-again? Only-on-Sunday-morning? No!)

*"...watching **daily** at my gates, waiting beside my door."*

This is what wisdom is saying:

Happy is that man, waiting beside my door daily,

...<u>that man is in a position where I could meet with him</u>!

Daily I'm bringing my life into a position *where I can receive from God, where I can be embraced of God,*

...so I can be a blessing in my neighborhood and to everyone around me,

...and so I can even go out of my way and begin to be a blessing to the whole world!

Isaiah 50:4

"The Lord God has given me the tongue of those who are taught"

And so you think,

'Well pastor Rudi, or pastor so-and-so, you're such a fortunate young man, God has given you the golden tongue, you know; that's your ministry, you've been given a golden tongue!'

Here's the secret,

"I am taught, that I may know how to sustain with the Word, him who is weary."

"Morning by morning He awakens my ear to hear, as those who are taught"

*"…waiting **daily** besides the gates of wisdom…"*

This Word of redemption is the gates of wisdom.

This Word of His grace and of His love is the wisdom of God!

It's the will of God revealed for this world!

So daily I'm waiting besides the gate,

I open the gate and I say,

'Wisdom, I'm ready to have an encounter with You,

…to receive Your impartation in my life,'

'...so I might begin to have the tongue of the learned,'

'...so I may know <u>how to sustain</u> with a word him who is weary and worn out.'

When we have that attitude released in our hearts, I'm telling you, *there is no stronghold,*

...no gates of hell that will prevail!

We will be able to take the spoil!

...to set the captives free!

...because we will walk in a new confidence!

...we will have confidence in the ability of His Word and of His love in us,

...to release people!

...to set the captives free!

Chapter 13

Abide in Him so you can bear much fruit!

John 15:1

"I am the true vine and My Father is the vinedresser"

I want you to see this picture:

Here we are; Jesus is planted over 2014 years ago. He is manifested in the flesh and is planted into the soil of this world. God has rooted Him into the soil of this world, and through His death He was cut off, *but His roots, His word, His truth, His life-giving-truth; that demonstration of His love, remains in this world.*

You know, you can cut that tree off, *but resurrection life will prevail,*

...that life and love will prevail!

...and suddenly that tree will begin to grow again!

And He says,

"Now you are the result of My growth, because you are like little branches now that is now growing forth from this vine.

Every one of you that have been linked to God through the Word of the Gospel, through understanding that gospel, through faith, through seeing accurately,

...through seeing and believing what God sees and believe happened in the work of redemption,

...through seeing and believing the love God has for you and for the whole world,

...you have clutched the hand of God and you have embraced His faith, and you have embraced His love,

...and you have entered into a covenant with God, so that now you can grow forth from Him."

He says,

"But My Father is a responsible farmer,

...My Father is not after bonsai trees, you know, perfectly manipulated and controlled little trees, just decoration,

...that's what religion is after, not God,

...No, He's after a harvest."

You see, God's not just going to sit back on the screen porch of His farm and look over His beautiful vineyard, *and think,*

'Well, wonderful!'

No! God has an eye for fruit!

He recognizes it!

...and He wants it!

He walks through His vineyard, *and He's looking for fruit.*

And we think now,

'God come on now, don't look so close, just leave me alone for a while, why are You always watching, why are You always out here inspecting my life.'

Listen, God has a right to expect fruit.

"You have been entrusted with much! Much will be required of you."

But, this is how God works,

I just want you to see this:

"Every branch of mine that bears no fruit..."

You see; it is possible to hang onto Jesus ***and bear no fruit.***

And then we read God say *He's going to cut you off,*

…and we think, 'oh, how terrible, He's going to cut me off into hell.'

But no, the Greek word there is the word **"*prune*."**

So, He is going to cut me to the heart, He's going to prune me through His Word, and through His love, and by His Spirit within me,

…He is going to challenge every dead thing in my life, every idol that produces death in my life!

He is going to speak a word straight into my spirit, and it is going to cut through every lie and deception,

…and what He does through His Word, through redemption truth, and through His love, is going to quicken me, and impart life to my spirit,

…so I can begin to produce and bear fruit!

The Word of God is sharper than any two-edged sword, *and it helps me!*

It cuts asunder ever thought and intent of the heart.

It brings every thought and every stronghold of the enemy into captivity *to the obedience **of** Christ,*

*…to **His obedience** that led to that cross,*

*…to the freedom that **His obedience** afforded me!*

*"You are already pruned; you are already clean, **by the Word's I have spoken to you**."*

(But if that doesn't work, if you refuse to yield to My truth, and My working within you,

…you will end up in a pile of sticks that have outlived their purpose and are only good to be thrown into the fire and burned.

He is saying that those thoughts of deception, lying against the truth of your redemption,

*…those deceptions **you cling to** and its various adverse consequences it results in,*

…and those various other adverse circumstances also,

…will destroy your life,

…if you don't allow the Word, if you don't allow His love, to prune you and clean you and keep you free!

*…because you see, **the truth is your defense**,*

…and now you have no defense against these things causing death in your life,

…because you rejected God's truth!)

"Abide in Me and I in you."

"As the branch cannot bear fruit by itself, so neither can you unless you abide in Me."

"By this my Father is glorified that you bear much fruit and so you are My disciples indeed."

"If My Word abides in you, you will speak forth what you desire and it will be born for you *by the power of My Father who is in Heaven (who rules over this natural world from that higher dimension, from that unseen realm of spirit reality and authority)"*

Where does much fruit come from?

From pruning!

From the Word!

From the truth of redemption!

From yielding to that truth!

…yielding to His love, yielding to Him!

"Every branch in Me that bears fruit, I will prune you so you can bear more fruit, so you can bear <u>much fruit</u>!"

God is not expecting pastor so-and-so alone *to bear much fruit!*

No, He expects you *to bear much fruit!*

God is not expecting pastor so-and-so to bear much fruit *in the ministry!*

No, He expects you to bear much fruit *in the ministry of reconciliation He has entrusted us all with!*

He expects every one, every individual, *to bear much fruit,*

"...because we have all received a faith of equal standing, of equal potential in Christ,"

But the key is that relationship,

...that abiding in Him,

...in His Word and in His love;

...in His truth,

...in the demonstration of His love in redemption,

...and in the truth of that redemption!

When He cuts, you might have to lose some of your leaves, *some of your vain glory,*

...swallow some of your fleshly pride and self-righteousness,

...some of the excuses you have been hiding behind,

...like Adam and Eve,

...but your life will become attractive if you have something real to offer!

...if your relationship with God is real!

...if your faith is alive!

...if you can tap into and minister from the power of God!

Your life will become attractive if your love-affair with God is real!

...and if your love is real!

...if you have real truth and love to offer!

...if you become a fountain in a dry and weary land where there is no water!

You will become a popular person when your life starts producing!

...but the word will mature you;

...it will mature your love so it doesn't go to your head,

...it will mature your spirit and it will mature your love *to the point where you don't care about yourself and about receiving accolades from others,*

...*all you care about is people,*

...*and all you care about is seeing people free!*

...*seeing them embrace God's redemption truth!*

...*and seeing them fall in love with Him!*

Hey, this thing, this salvation Jesus died for *is not just about us!*

We have to see the chicken in the egg in the Word of God, *not just the egg.*

"...<u>seed to the sower</u> and not just bread for food!"

...*or all you will end up with is a bunch of old chickens producing a few eggs for food,*

Ha... ha... ha...

...*and far and few between at that!*

Hebrews 5:11

*"**About this we have much to say <u>but</u>** it is hard to explain, **<u>since</u> you have become dull of hearing**."*

"By this time <u>you ought to be teachers</u>!"

Paul is not saying, *'**I don't want to teach you**,'*

...but by this time you should be teachers yourselves!

That means every Word that I teach you; I want you to go and teach other's also!

Father, thank you that You have never considered any one of us after a mere human point of view,

...but You have always considered us after the truth of who we really are, **of who You know us to be in You**,

...and therefore after our full potential as well!

Thank you that You see us as qualified already!

Lacking nothing!

You have always considered us complete in Christ Jesus!

And You loved us while we were yet sinners,

...and living empty, barren lives, with no real purpose worth living for!

But Father thank you that You gave us *a purpose and a life worth living!*

...a life of infinite, eternal value!

...a life that can make a difference in this world!

...not just in humanistic terms, you know, by making this world a better place to merely exist in, no!

...but making a real difference!

...by making this world actually better, by redeeming our friends and our neighbors back out of the hands of the enemy!

Thank you Father God!

Amen!

In closing, I urge you to get yourself a copy of *"The Mirror Bible"* available online at: www.friendsofthemirror.com or at www.amazon.com and several other book sellers.

If you want me or someone a part of our team to come to where you are, *anywhere in the world,* and give a talk or teach you and some of your friends *about the gospel message and these redemption realities,* simply contact us at www.livingwordintl.com ...you can always find me on www.facebook.com

If your life has changed as a result of reading this book, *please write to me and let me know.*

I would love to share your joy,

...so that my joy in writing this book may be full!

That which was from the beginning,

which we have heard
(with our spiritual ears),
which we have seen
(with our spiritual eyes),
which we have looked upon
(beheld, focused our attention upon),
and which our hands have also handled
(which we have also experienced),

concerning the Word of life,

we declare to you,

that you also may have this fellowship with us;

and truly our fellowship is with the Father and with His Son Jesus Christ.

And these things we write to you **that your joy may be full.**

– 1 John 1:1-4

About the Author

Rudi & Carmen Louw together oversee and pastor a church: Living Word International

They also travel and minister both locally and internationally.

Rudi was born and raised in the country of South Africa, while Carmen grew up in Cortland, New York.

They function in the ministry of reconciliation (2Corinthians 5:18-21) and flow strongly in the gifts of the Holy Spirit and His anointing to teach, preach, prophecy, heal and whatever is needed to touch people's lives with the reality of God's love and power.

God has given them keen insight into what He has to say to mankind in the work of redemption,

...concerning the revelation of, and restoration of humanity's true identity,

...and therefore they emphasize THE GOSPEL; IN CHRIST REALITIES; the GRACE of God; the WORD OF RIGHTEOUSNESS *and all such eternal truths essential to salvation and living of the CHRIST-LIFE.*

They have been granted this wisdom and revelation into the knowledge of God by the resurrected Spirit of Jesus Christ, *to establish and strengthen believers in the faith of God, and to activate them in ministering to others.*

Not only are people set free from the poison and bondage of sin, condemnation and all kinds of intimidation, (upheld, strengthened and reinforced by age old religious ideas born out of ignorance,) **but many are brought into a closer more intimate relationship with Father God, as Daddy**, through accurate teaching, and unveiling of the gospel message, prophetic words, healings and miracles.

Rudi & Carmen are closely knitted together with many other effective Christians, church fellowships, and groups of believers who share the same revelation and passion.

www.ingramcontent.com/pod-product-compliance
Lightning Source LLC
Chambersburg PA
CBHW071119090426
42736CB00012B/1953